< CODER >
ACADEMY

First American Edition 2017
Kane Miller, A Division of EDC Publishing

Text © 2017 Sean McManus
Design and layout © 2017 Quarto Publishing plc

For information contact:
Kane Miller, A Division of EDC Publishing
5402 S 122nd E Ave
Tulsa, OK 74146
www.kanemiller.com
www.myubam.com

Library of Congress Control Number: 2017930981

Scratch is developed by the Lifelong Kindergarten Group
at the MIT Media Lab. See http://scratch.mit.edu

Printed in China

ISBN: 978-1-61067-600-7

4 5 6 7 8 9 10

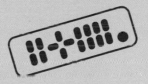

< CODER >
ACADEMY

WRITTEN BY
SEAN McMANUS

ILLUSTRATED BY
ROSAN MAGAR

Kane Miller
A DIVISION OF EDC PUBLISHING

‹CONTENTS›

GETTING TO KNOW CODE

WELCOME TO CODER ACADEMY!

Congratulations! You have now joined Coder Academy, where you will learn all about what it takes to become a coder.

Imagine an alien came to visit. If you wanted to tell it what to do, you'd have to learn its language first. It's similar with computers. To give them instructions or information, you need to write in a way they can understand. Coding is all about writing instructions and information in a computer language.

Almost anywhere you go, you're surrounded by computer code running on tiny chips. For example, code is used in phones, video games, GPS, trains, heating systems and factories.

As you work your way through the book, you'll learn about what a coder needs to be able to do. This includes:

- Understanding different computer languages, such as Scratch.
- Writing simple commands for a computer to follow.
- Designing computer art for games and programs.
- Building web pages and websites using HTML.

Your first task is to fill in your Trainee Coder login.

If you can't get a program to work, carefully check it against the book for any differences. With computer code, even small changes can stop things from working. If you still can't get it to work, you can download an example from the author's website at www.sean.co.uk/books/coder.

NAME:

PASSWORD:

LOGIN

MEET THE
CODERS

At the Academy, you'll train in a number of skills that are used to make video games, animation and music, and simple web pages.

You'll need to complete a number of training tasks to earn your certificates and qualify in each area. When you have fully qualified, you can graduate from Coder Academy, and you will have taken the first steps toward becoming a coder—one day, you may be able to write a program that controls a robot or that sends an astronaut into space!

CODERS

write instructions for the computer to tell it what to do. They need to think clearly, and be precise. A lot of their time is spent testing programs and making sure they work.

COMPUTER ARTISTS

create the images used in computer software, including designing characters and animations for games. Sometimes they design icons and buttons, too.

COMPUTER MUSICIANS

make music using software. They might create the soundtrack for a computer game, invent musical software, or use the computer to make music for a movie or album.

WEBSITE DEVELOPERS

create the code for websites, using the languages HTML and CSS. They sometimes work with website content creators, who write the articles for the website.

WHAT IS CODING?

It is the coder's job to tell the computer what to do. The information the computer needs to carry out a task has to be given in a way the computer can understand—in computer language, or code.

When the coder is writing the instructions for a program, even the simplest tasks have to be clearly set out. For example, in an art program the computer needs to know how to move the cursor around on the screen and to recognize the tools and colors being used, as well as more complex tasks. So the art program must contain the computer code on how to do all of these things.

Even computers that respond to spoken instructions need to use code to understand what a voice is telling them to do.

I-SPY CODING

All kinds of devices use computer code to carry out tasks. Connect the four devices with the code tasks below. Some devices can do more than one task.

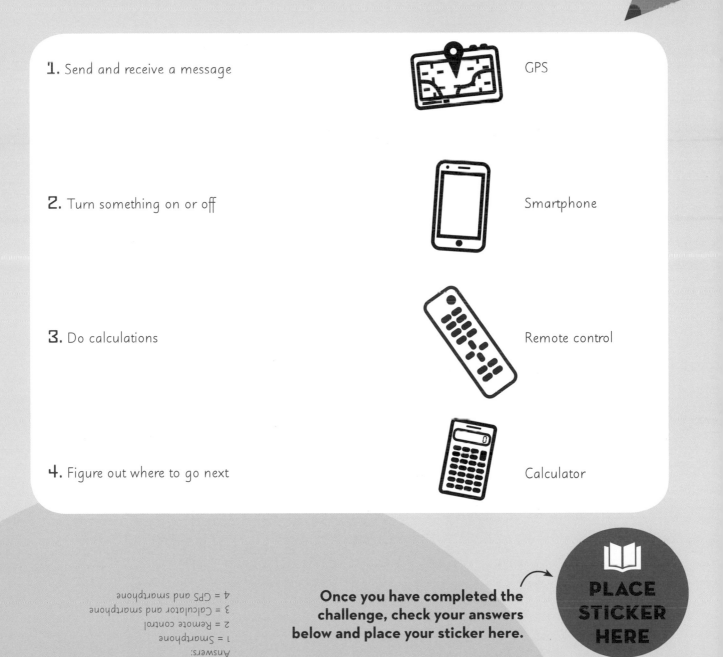

1. Send and receive a message · GPS

2. Turn something on or off · Smartphone

3. Do calculations · Remote control

4. Figure out where to go next · Calculator

Once you have completed the challenge, check your answers below and place your sticker here.

PLACE STICKER HERE

TASK COMPLETE

THINK LIKE —A CODER—

To write instructions in computer language, a coder needs to be precise and accurate. They also need to be able to work through each problem step-by-step, like a computer does. You are going to give a friend simple instructions to complete a task. Can you think like a coder?

ROBOT PROGRAMMING CHALLENGE

You will need: two pencils, two pieces of paper, a friend

1. Decide who will be the robot and who will be the programmer. Take a piece of paper and a pencil each and sit back-to-back, so that neither of you can see what the other is doing.

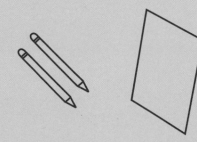

2. The programmer draws a picture on their piece of paper, using only straight lines and circles. The drawing could be a person, a car, a house, or anything else you like.

3. Without telling the robot what it is, the programmer gives the robot instructions for drawing the same picture, following these rules:

* The programmer can only tell the robot to draw straight lines or circles.

* The programmer must tell the robot how long or short to make the lines and circles, and where to draw them on the paper.

4. The robot must follow the instructions precisely to draw the picture.

When you've finished, compare the two pictures. How similar are they?

Now swap roles and draw a different picture. Agree on some new commands between you, to make drawing the shapes easier.

Once you have completed the challenge, place your sticker here.

PLACE STICKER HERE

TASK COMPLETE

BINARY BASICS

It is useful to understand a number system called "binary" if you want to become a coder. This is because computers use binary to store and process information. Words, pictures, music and colors are all stored using binary.

Binary is a place-value system. This means that the position of the digits in the number tells you how much it is worth. In binary, the value of the digit to the left is twice as much as the value of the digit to the right—and binary can go on like this forever! A binary number only has 0s or 1s. It can look like this: 10000001. This number equals 129. The number 11100111 equals 231.

Find out below how this system works.

The digits **0** and **1** act like switches; **0** means "off" and **1** means "on." Look at the example to the right.

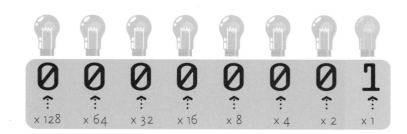

The computer switches the value of x 1 "on," and switches everything else "off." Add all the "on" values together to get the number. In this example, x 1 is switched "on" and everything else is switched "off." So, **0+0+0+0+0+0+0+1 = 1**. Look at another binary number and apply the same rule to get the answer:

Switch "on" the value of x 2 and the value of x 1, and switch everything else "off."
So, **0+0+0+0+0+0+2+1 = 3**.

Practice the skills you learned on page 14 and decode the binary below to unlock some computing facts.

1. Binary is also sometimes known as Base **00000010.**

DECODE:

2. The Asimo robot can walk and is as tall as an adult. It weighs **01101010** lb.

DECODE:

3. There are **00110100** computers that control the systems on the International Space Station.

DECODE:

4. A byte is eight binary digits, or bits. A nybble is **00000100** bits.

DECODE:

Answers:
1 = 2 [Base 2]
2 = 106 lb
3 = 52
4 = 4

Once you have completed the challenge, check your answers below and then place your sticker here.

PLACE STICKER HERE

TASK COMPLETE

COMPUTER LANGUAGES

Russian Privet!

French Salut!

Spanish ¡Hola!

What languages can you think of? Maybe you or someone you know can speak French, German, Spanish or Mandarin Chinese.

Computer systems have their own languages. They aren't meant to be spoken by people, but to give a computer instructions in a way that it can understand.

Before coders make a program or give a computer information, they must select the best computer language to use. Some languages are good for many jobs, but others can only do one thing!

Look at the chart below to see how coders use different computer languages. The computer languages can be used in many ways other than those listed here.

HTML	HTML is used for the information on a website.
C++	C++ is used to make superfast games for consoles and desktops.
JAVASCRIPT	JavaScript makes websites interactive, so that they can move images around and users can play games. It is also used for making smartphone and computer games.
SCRATCH	You can create desktop computer games, stories and animations using Scratch. It is one of the easiest of all programming languages.
SWIFT	Swift was invented by Apple. It is used to make apps for Apple's phones and tablets.
JAVA	A coder creating an app for Android devices will use a version of Java. This language is also used in machines that have a tiny computer in them, such as hospital equipment.
PYTHON	Python can be used with a Raspberry Pi, a playing-card-sized computer, to make robots. It can also be used to make desktop computer games.

MATCH THE LANGUAGE

Coders need to know which language to use for different programs. Match the five computer languages with what they can be used to make. Some computer languages can be matched more than once.

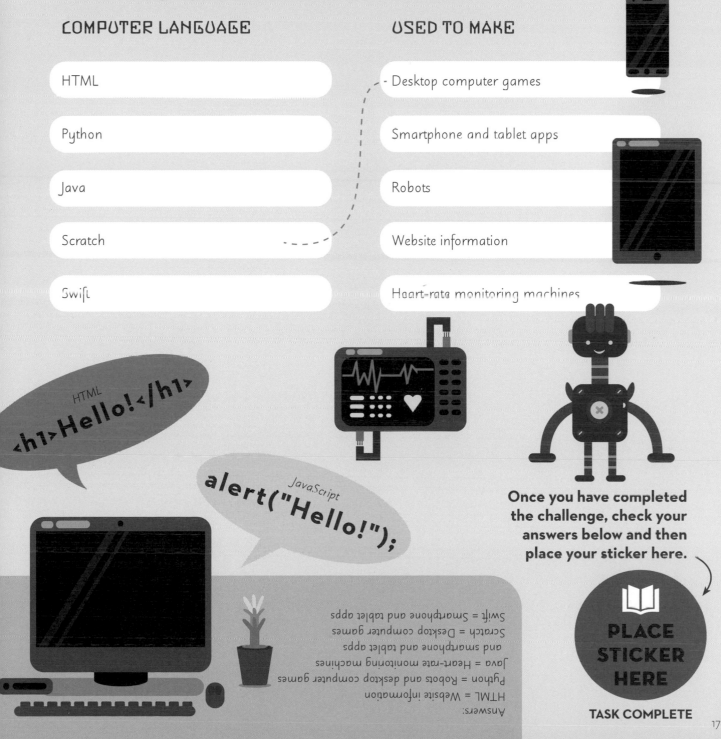

COMPUTER LANGUAGE

HTML

Python

Java

Scratch

Swift

USED TO MAKE

Desktop computer games

Smartphone and tablet apps

Robots

Website information

Heart-rate monitoring machines

HTML
<h1>Hello!</h1>

JavaScript
alert("Hello!");

Once you have completed the challenge, check your answers below and then place your sticker here.

Answers:
HTML = Website information
Python = Robots and desktop computer games
Java = Heart-rate monitoring machines and smartphone and tablet apps
Scratch = Desktop computer games
Swift = Smartphone and tablet apps

PLACE STICKER HERE

TASK COMPLETE

17

START FROM —SCRATCH—

A good way to begin your training as a coder is to get started with Scratch.

Scratch is a simple computer language that will teach you the basics of coding. It is free to use. With it, you can choose from a set of commands to make stories, animations and even your very own game!

To use Scratch, visit the website at **scratch.mit.edu** and click "Create" at the top. If you set up an account, you can save your programs automatically. Ask an adult to help you with this. The latest version of Scratch is called Scratch 3. The previous versions of Scratch, Scratch 1.4 and Scratch 2.0, are still available to download.

In Scratch, you create simple games and animations using blocks that snap together (a bit like a jigsaw puzzle piece) to create scripts. If you look at the Scratch screen on the opposite page, you will find out more about how blocks work.

As you work through this book, you will create your own Scratch projects. Build the script in the order that you see it on the page. Look at the color of each block on the page to find it in Scratch—for example, when you need a dark blue block, you will find it by clicking the Motion button, which is also dark blue.

CODER INFO

Images you can move are called sprites. Sprites can be found in the Sprite List in Scratch, or you can create your own.

Below is what you will see on the screen when you open Scratch. Refer back to this information when you begin the first Scratch activity on page 22.

BUTTONS

Instructions in Scratch are called blocks. Blocks can be used to change the size of your sprite, how it will move and where it will go. Use the buttons to choose different types of blocks.

FILE MENU

Make an account to save your Scratch projects online. You can also download them to your computer. Use the File menu to save your work.

TABS

There are three tabs to switch between. Choose blocks (instructions) from the **Code** tab. The **Costumes** tab allows you to change how your sprite looks. Find music to accompany your games and animations using the **Sounds** tab.

STAGE

See your animations and games come to life here.

ADD EXTENSION

Add more blocks to Scratch here.

BLOCKS PALETTE

Find the blocks to use in scripts here.

CODE AREA

Scratch programs are called scripts. Click on your chosen block from the Blocks Palette, then drag and drop it in the Code Area.

SPRITE LIST

With the Choose a Sprite button, you can choose from lots of different kinds of sprites, and even design your own characters.

PLOT COORDINATES

If you want to create a piece of computer art or a game, you need to know how to tell the computer where to put things. The way you do that is using coordinates—two numbers that identify a particular point on the screen. You might have come across coordinates on maps or graphs before.

The x number is used for the distance from left to right across the screen. The easy way to remember it is that "x is across" (and it's also "a cross!"). The y number is used for the distance up and down the screen.

Both the x and y numbers are measured from the middle of the screen, where x is 0 and y is 0. The x numbers are positive on the right, and negative on the left. The y numbers are positive at the top, and negative at the bottom.

A coordinate is the point where x and y meet. Look at the point marked on the chart. The x line (or axis) is 150, and the y line is 100. That means the coordinates are 150, 100.

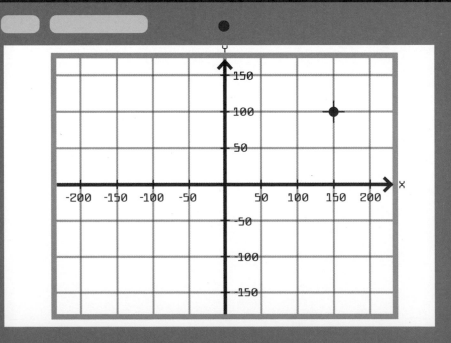

WHERE AM I?

Figure out the coordinates of each character in the pictures below. Use the chart on page 20 as a guide. You will need to be able to do this when you create your first game in Scratch on the next page.

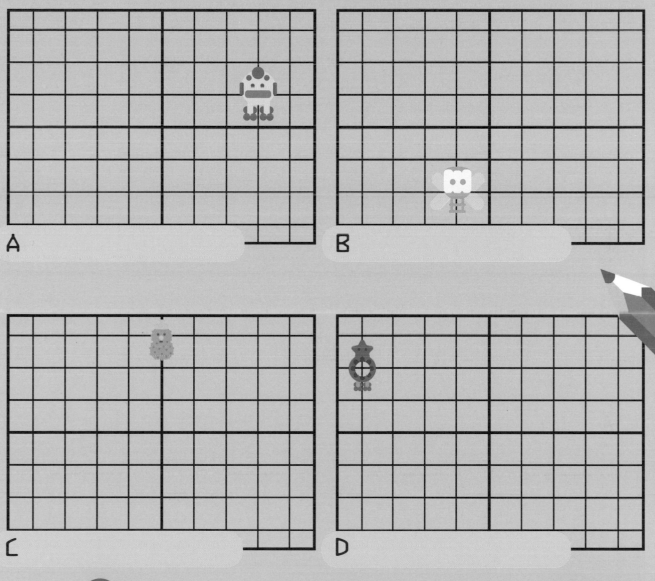

A

B

C

D

Once you have completed the challenge, check your answers below and then place your sticker here.

PLACE STICKER HERE

TASK COMPLETE

Answers: A = 150, 50; B = -50, -100; C = 0, 150; D = -200, 100.

CODE COORDINATES

Now you are ready to start using Scratch. You are going to build a script, using a set of blocks, to help a cat hunt down a ghost. Open up Scratch to see the Scratch screen (see page 19 for help). It may seem a bit complicated, but once you get started, it is very easy to use. The cat is the default sprite, so will be in the Sprite List already.

MAKE THE CAT'S CODE

when | space ▼ | key pressed

1. The block colors tell you where to find the blocks. The first block is yellow, so click the yellow **Events** button. The **Events** blocks start a script when something happens. Find the **when space key pressed** block in the Blocks Palette. This block will start your script when you press the space key on your keyboard. Click the block and drag it into the Code Area.

when | space ▼ | key pressed
set size to (50)%

2. The second block is purple, so click the purple **Looks** button. The **Looks** blocks control the appearance of your sprite. Find the **set size to 100%** block. This controls the size of your sprite. Drag it into the Code Area. Drop it close enough under the yellow block so they snap together. Click the white hole in the purple block and use the keyboard to change the number from 100 to 50. This will make your sprite smaller when the script runs.

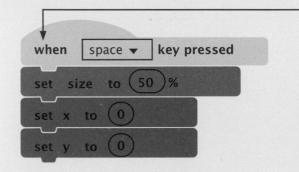

when | space ▼ | key pressed
set size to (50)%
set x to (0)
set y to (0)

3. Click the blue **Motion** button. The **Motion** blocks let you control how your sprite moves across the Stage. Add the **set x to 0** and **set y to 0** blocks to the script, making sure they snap together. Change the numbers in the blue **Motion** blocks. This action lets you change the coordinates of your sprite on the Stage. Can you figure out the x and y positions to put the cat in the top right corner?

4. Click the Stage and press the space key to see the cat move to the x and y coordinates you chose.

MAKE THE GHOST'S CODE

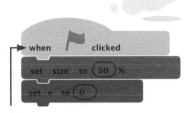

1. Click the **Choose a Sprite** button in the bottom right of the Sprite List. Find the **Fantasy** category. Find the ghost and click it. In the Sprite List, make sure the ghost is selected.

2. Click the **Events** button and add the **when green flag clicked** block to the Code Area. From the **Looks** section, choose the **set size to 100%** block. Add it to the Code Area, then change the number to 50.

3. Click the **Motion** button and choose a **set x to 0** block. Add it to the Code Area.

4. Click the **Operators** button. The blocks in this section allow you to do calculations and change pieces of text. Select the **pick random 1 to 10** block, and drop it on top of the number in the **set x to 0** block in the Code Area.

5. The **pick random** block is like rolling a dice, except there are hundreds of numbers, not just six. Change the numbers in the **pick random 1 to 10** block to -200 and 200. This will randomize the x coordinate of the ghost.

6. Add a **set y to 0** block with a **pick random 1 to 10** block in the same way. Change the numbers to -140 and 140. This will randomize the y coordinate of the ghost.

PLAY THE GAME

Now you're ready to play! Click the green flag above the Stage and the ghost will move somewhere random. Click the cat in the Sprite List and change the numbers in the cat's code. Click the Stage and press space. Did the cat catch the ghost? If not, change its coordinates, click the Stage and press space again. How many turns does it take the cat to catch the ghost?

Once you have completed the challenge, place your sticker here.

PLACE STICKER HERE

TASK COMPLETE

23

STEP-BY-STEP

Sometimes you need a computer to repeat the same instructions many times. What's the clearest and simplest way to tell the computer to do that? Let's find out.

**Here are two sets of instructions for the same dance.
Which set is easier to follow? Try them both out and see!**

SET 1

- Step to the left
- Step to the left
- Step to the left
- Step to the left
- Step to the right
- Step to the right
- Step to the right
- Step to the right
- Step backward
- Step backward
- Step backward
- Step backward
- Step forward
- Step forward
- Step forward
- Step forward

SET 2

- Step to the left, four times
- Step to the right, four times
- Step backward, four times
- Step forward, four times

You probably found Set 2 much easier! This shows how we can make our programs easier to write, and easier to understand. If we want a Scratch sprite to do the same thing several times, we can use a **repeat** block to tell it how many times.

INVENT A DANCE

On the next two pages, you will code a dance for a sprite in Scratch. Use the table below to plan the commands for the computer to follow. Circle the direction arrow, then write in the number of steps for the sprite to take. Your sprite can go forward, backward, left or right. In the program, the steps need to be multiples of 4, so work that out here, too.

WHICH DIRECTION?				HOW MANY STEPS?	MULTIPLY BY 4
▶ RIGHT	▼ DOWN *(circled)*	◀ LEFT	▲ UP	4	16
▶ RIGHT	▼ DOWN	◀ LEFT	▲ UP		
▶ RIGHT	▼ DOWN	◀ LEFT	▲ UP		
▶ RIGHT	▼ DOWN	◀ LEFT	▲ UP		
▶ RIGHT	▼ DOWN	◀ LEFT	▲ UP		
▶ RIGHT	▼ DOWN	◀ LEFT	▲ UP		
▶ RIGHT	▼ DOWN	◀ LEFT	▲ UP		
▶ RIGHT	▼ DOWN	◀ LEFT	▲ UP		
▶ RIGHT	▼ DOWN	◀ LEFT	▲ UP		

Once you have completed the challenge, place your sticker here.

PLACE STICKER HERE

TASK COMPLETE

25

MAKE A
SPRITE DANCE

On page 25, you planned a set of dance steps using as few instructions as possible.
In Scratch, you can repeat instructions using the **repeat 10** block (on page 29, you use
a **forever** block to repeat instructions endlessly). Now, put your dance steps into code.

SET UP YOUR SPRITE

1. Start a new Scratch project. Click the **Choose a Sprite** button in the bottom right of the Sprite List. Go to the Dance category, and click Cassy Dance.

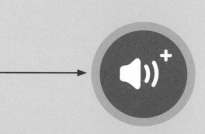

2. Click the **Sounds** tab. Click the speaker icon in the bottom left. Go to the Loops category, and add your favorite tune. The tune in this code is "eggs."

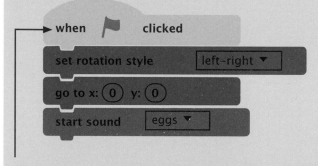

3. Click the **Code** tab and add this code to your sprite.

4. Right-click the cat in the Sprite List, and click delete to remove it.

When you see a sprite move, you are looking at different pictures of the sprite (see pages 40–41). Each picture is called a costume. Cassy has four costumes. For each step in the dance, we want her to perform all four of her body movements.

ADD YOUR DANCE STEPS

Below you can see the blocks you need to add to your script to make Cassy take one dance step in each direction.

1. Start with the first row of your table on page 25. Add the blocks for the step direction—right, left, up or down—to your script.

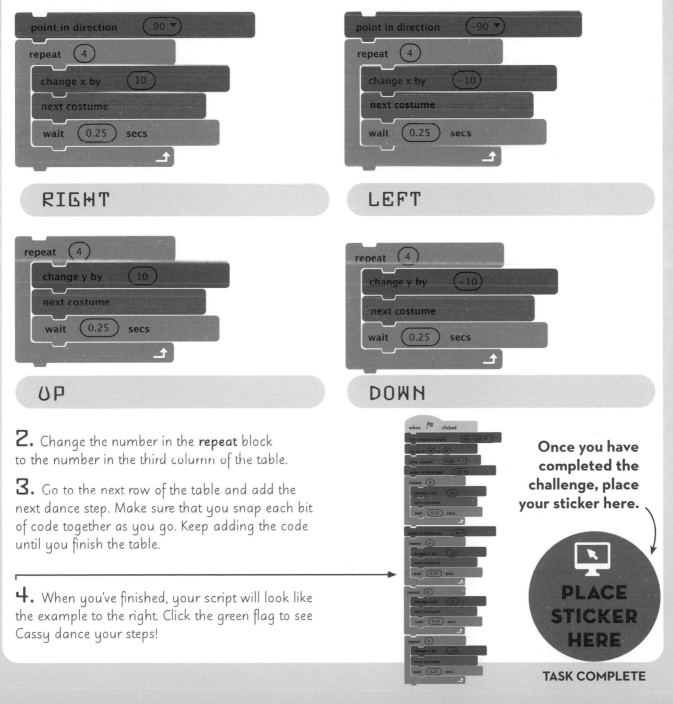

| point in direction 90 ▼ |
| repeat 4 |
| change x by 10 |
| next costume |
| wait 0.25 secs |

RIGHT

| point in direction -90 ▼ |
| repeat 4 |
| change x by -10 |
| next costume |
| wait 0.25 secs |

LEFT

| repeat 4 |
| change y by 10 |
| next costume |
| wait 0.25 secs |

UP

| repeat 4 |
| change y by -10 |
| next costume |
| wait 0.25 secs |

DOWN

2. Change the number in the **repeat** block to the number in the third column of the table.

3. Go to the next row of the table and add the next dance step. Make sure that you snap each bit of code together as you go. Keep adding the code until you finish the table.

4. When you've finished, your script will look like the example to the right. Click the green flag to see Cassy dance your steps!

Once you have completed the challenge, place your sticker here.

PLACE STICKER HERE

TASK COMPLETE

27

VARIABLES

Write a shopping list of several items and give each item a price. You are going to make a program in Scratch that uses something called a variable to show both the total value of your shopping list, and the number of items on the list.

MAKING A VARIABLE FOR A SHOPPING LIST CALCULATOR

To remember information, computers use variables. These are like boxes to put information in. You might have a variable called "score" to remember a player's score in a game, for example. You can change the number of the score during the game. It's called a variable because it can vary (or change). Variables can be used to remember words or numbers. Here is how to create a variable in Scratch:

1. Start a new project in Scratch.

2. Click the **Variables** button, then choose **Make a Variable**.

3. Name the variable "total" and click **OK**. Make another variable, called "number of items."

4. Uncheck the boxes beside "total" and "number of items" in the Blocks Palette. This hides them on the Stage.

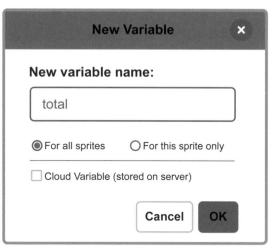

In the **Variables** part of the Blocks Palette, you'll find blocks to change your variables. You will use the drop-down box in these blocks to select the variable you need to add to the script—either "total" or "number of items." Now you are ready to build your shopping list calculator.

5. Add this script to your cat sprite:

A Use the drop-down box to select the variable needed.

B Set both variables to zero at the start.

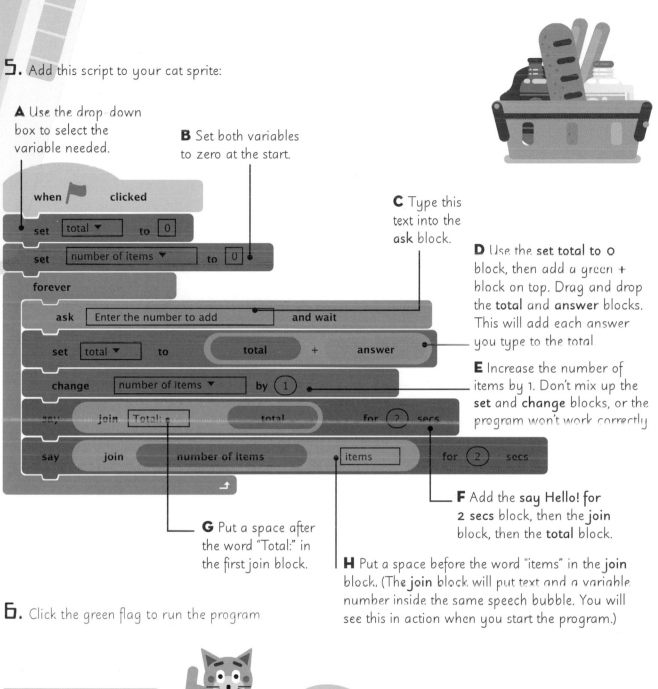

C Type this text into the **ask** block.

D Use the **set total to 0** block, then add a green **+** block on top. Drag and drop the **total** and **answer** blocks. This will add each answer you type to the total.

E Increase the number of items by 1. Don't mix up the **set** and **change** blocks, or the program won't work correctly.

```
when 🏳 clicked
set total ▼ to 0
set number of items ▼ to 0
forever
    ask Enter the number to add and wait
    set total ▼ to ( total + answer )
    change number of items ▼ by (1)
    say join Total: total for (2) secs
    say join number of items items for (2) secs
```

F Add the **say Hello! for 2 secs** block, then the **join** block, then the **total** block.

G Put a space after the word "Total:" in the first join block.

H Put a space before the word "items" in the **join** block. (The **join** block will put text and a variable number inside the same speech bubble. You will see this in action when you start the program.)

6. Click the green flag to run the program

Enter the number to add

7. Using the shopping list you wrote, type the price of each item into the cat's text box on the Stage. The program will add up the total and will keep track of the number of items in the list.

Once you have completed the challenge, place your sticker here.

PLACE STICKER HERE

TASK COMPLETE

FLOW CHARTS

Before coders write a program, they sometimes make a flow chart of the instructions. The coder uses it to check that all the steps are in the right places and in the correct order. See how a flow chart works by playing this game.

You read a flow chart from the top and follow the arrows.

The diamond boxes are where the computer decides which path to follow.

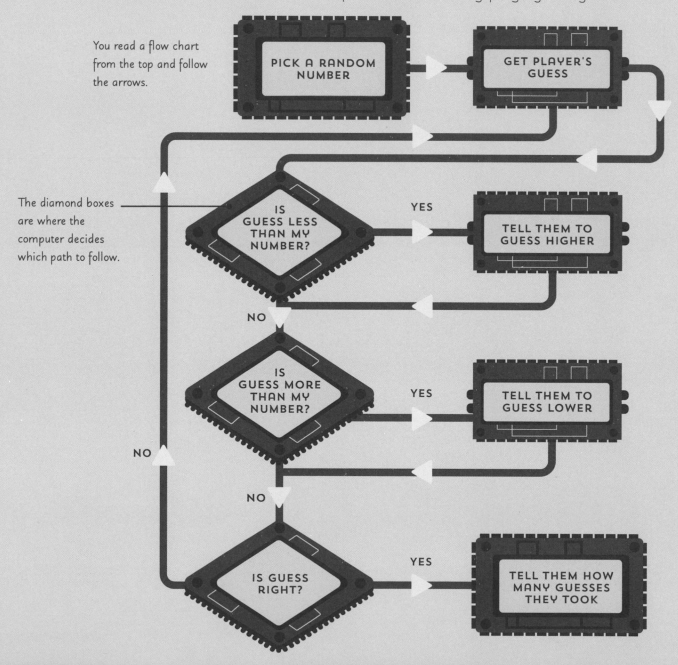

PICK A RANDOM NUMBER

GET PLAYER'S GUESS

IS GUESS LESS THAN MY NUMBER?

YES → TELL THEM TO GUESS HIGHER

NO

IS GUESS MORE THAN MY NUMBER?

YES → TELL THEM TO GUESS LOWER

NO

NO

IS GUESS RIGHT?

YES → TELL THEM HOW MANY GUESSES THEY TOOK

GUESS THE NUMBER

The flow chart on page 30 shows the instructions for a game program where players guess a number chosen by the computer. But does it work? Use a dice to pick a random number for the computer and a guess for the player. Then start at the top of the flow chart and use a pen to draw the path through it. Try several times with different numbers and different colored markers. How does the path change if you guess high, low or correct?

You will need: colored markers, a dice

MARKER COLOR	COMPUTER NUMBER	PLAYER'S GUESS	PLAYER NUMBER WAS HIGH, LOW OR CORRECT?

Once you have completed the challenge, place your sticker here.

PLACE STICKER HERE

TASK COMPLETE

MAKING DECISIONS

On pages 30—31, you used a flow chart to process a decision. Remember this part of the flow chart?

In Scratch, you use the **if ... then** bracket to do this. The computer decides whether or not to carry out the instructions inside the bracket. If not, they're ignored. **If ... then** brackets can be used for many different types of decision making.

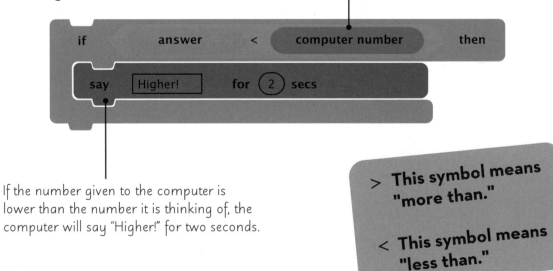

IS GUESS LESS THAN MY NUMBER?

YES

TELL THEM TO GUESS HIGHER

NO

In this example, a player is trying to guess the number that the computer is holding. The diamond hole of the bracket checks if the answer given is lower than the number that the computer is thinking of.

if answer < computer number then

say Higher! for (2) secs

If the number given to the computer is lower than the number it is thinking of, the computer will say "Higher!" for two seconds.

> **This symbol means "more than."**

< **This symbol means "less than."**

HIGHER OR LOWER GAME

The sprite is thinking of a number between 1 and 100. The aim of the game is to guess the number in the fewest tries possible.

1. Start a new project in Scratch. Make **Variables** and call them "guesses" and "computer number." Uncheck the boxes beside each variable in the Blocks Palette to hide them on the Stage, otherwise players will see the answer!

2. Add this script to your cat sprite:

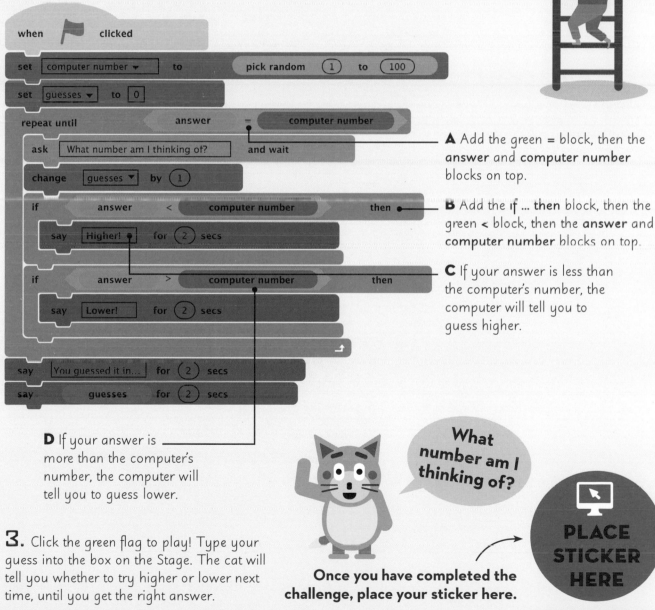

A Add the green = block, then the **answer** and **computer number** blocks on top.

B Add the if ... then block, then the green < block, then the **answer** and **computer number** blocks on top.

C If your answer is less than the computer's number, the computer will tell you to guess higher.

D If your answer is more than the computer's number, the computer will tell you to guess lower.

3. Click the green flag to play! Type your guess into the box on the Stage. The cat will tell you whether to try higher or lower next time, until you get the right answer.

What number am I thinking of?

Once you have completed the challenge, place your sticker here.

PLACE STICKER HERE

TASK COMPLETE

33

USING BROADCASTS

Computer game coders often need the characters they program to coordinate with each other, and do things on the screen at the same time. In Scratch, a sprite can send a message, called a broadcast, that tells the other sprites to run their scripts. Here's an example program: when you click the cat, it tells the other sprites to move.

1. Start a new project in Scratch. Add two new sprites: a pair of glasses and a hat. Drag them on the Stage and put them on the cat.

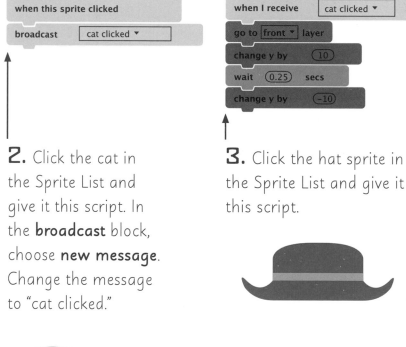

2. Click the cat in the Sprite List and give it this script. In the **broadcast** block, choose **new message**. Change the message to "cat clicked."

3. Click the hat sprite in the Sprite List and give it this script.

4. Click the glasses sprite in the Sprite List and give it this script.

5. Click the cat on the Stage. It will send the message "cat clicked" to the other sprites. The other sprites will receive the message, and the hat will jump, and the glasses will tilt!

PLACE STICKER HERE

Once you have completed the challenge, place your sticker here.

TASK COMPLETE

CONGRATULATIONS! You are now a ...

QUALIFIED CODER

CODER NAME:

_____

The above-named coder is qualified to be a

CODER

and to build games and other programs in Scratch.

Coder Academy would like to wish you every success in your coding career! GOOD LUCK.

QUALIFICATION DATE:

_____

DESIGN A CHARACTER

Animators create computer game characters. Although they need to draw well, they also need to give a lot of thought to the characters they design. The best characters have features that the player likes, making the player want to help them win in a game.

Pick three of your favorite characters. The characters could be from a book, movie or game. In the box below, write down why you like them. Is it because they are fun, brave, scary—or something else?

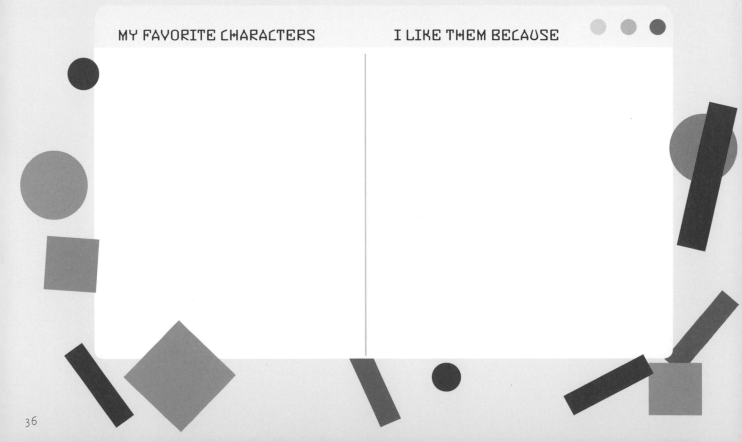

MY FAVORITE CHARACTERS	I LIKE THEM BECAUSE

INVENT A CHARACTER

Use this space to design a character using the stickers in the back of the book. Use squares, rectangles and circles for the basic shape of your character, then add details and color using colored pens or pencils. If you run out of stickers, draw extra squares, rectangles and circles.

Once you have completed the challenge, place your sticker here.

PLACE STICKER HERE

TASK COMPLETE

CREATE A CHARACTER

You are going to use your character design from page 37 to make your very own sprite in Scratch. You can have lots of fun playing around with different sprites, and watching your creations come to life! To create a new sprite, hover over the **Choose a Sprite** button in the Sprite List, and click **Paint**. Here's what you will see when you open the Paint Editor:

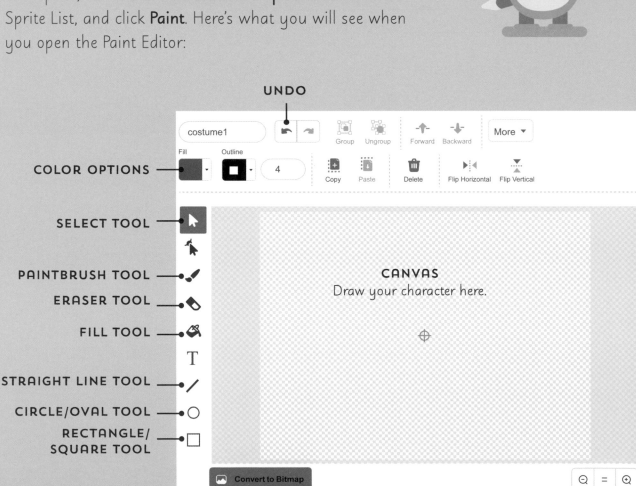

UNDO

COLOR OPTIONS

SELECT TOOL

PAINTBRUSH TOOL

ERASER TOOL

FILL TOOL

STRAIGHT LINE TOOL

CIRCLE/OVAL TOOL

RECTANGLE/
SQUARE TOOL

USING THE PAINT EDITOR

You can draw **straight lines**, **circles**, **squares** and **rectangles** in the same way: select the tool for the shape you need, then click the canvas, hold the mouse button down and drag the cursor. Release the mouse button when the shape is the right size.

You can click a shape and move it immediately after drawing it. The curved arrow under the shape is a **rotate** control: click it, hold the mouse button down and move your mouse to rotate, or turn, your shape.

To use the **paintbrush** or **eraser** tools, click the tool, hold the mouse button down on the canvas and move the mouse.

Click **undo** if you make a mistake.

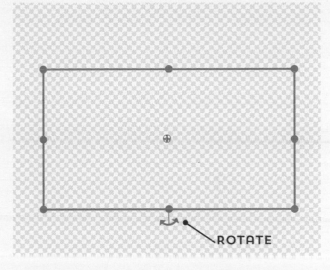

ROTATE

To create a sprite in Scratch using your sticker design on page 37, use the **circle** and **rectangle/square** tools to create the shapes that make up your character. If you placed stickers on top of each other, start with the shapes at the back first. Use the **select** tool, then click a shape and you can move it, rotate it, and change its color. This helps to line everything up perfectly. Use the **paintbrush** tool to draw any details you added to your sticker design. Try to draw your shape over the target in the middle of the canvas. This will make sure your sprite is positioned correctly in your games.

Once you have completed the challenge, place your sticker here.

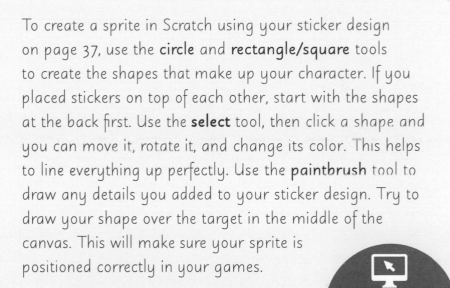

PLACE
STICKER
HERE

TASK COMPLETE

39

—ANIMATE—
A CHARACTER

Computer artists animate their characters so that they move or change expression. Animation tricks your eyes into seeing movement by flashing a row of still pictures in front of them. Try out this paper animation to see how it works.

You will need: a letter-sized sheet of paper, a felt-tip pen, a long pencil

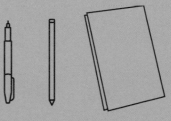

1. Fold the paper in half from top to bottom, then unfold. Using only circles, rectangles and squares, draw a picture on the bottom half using a felt-tip pen. Don't draw too close to the fold!

2. Fold the top half of the paper over again so that it covers your drawing. Press the front so your drawing inside is visible and trace over it, making a few small changes.

3. Place the pencil at the open edge of the paper. Roll the top sheet of the paper around the pencil, making sure it's tight.

4. Quickly roll the pencil up and down to see your animation!

MAKE YOUR MOVING SPRITE

Use your paper animation design to create a moving sprite in Scratch.

1. Hover over the **Choose a Sprite** button in the Sprite List, and click **Paint.**

2. Use the Paint Editor to recreate the first image from your paper animation on page 40.

4. Click the copy of your sprite and edit it in the Paint Editor, making small changes so that it matches the second picture from your paper animation. Remember you can use the **eraser** tool to remove the parts of the sprite that you need to change.

5. Turn to page 42 to code your animated sprite into a game.

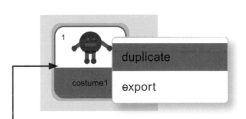

3. Right-click on the small picture of the sprite you have made to the left of the Paint Editor. Click duplicate—this will make a copy of the sprite's costume.

Once you have completed the challenge, place your sticker here.

PLACE STICKER HERE

TASK COMPLETE

CODE A CHARACTER

Now that you have designed and created a sprite, you are going to code a game for your character to star in. The aim of the game is to use the cursor keys to avoid things falling from the sky.

1. Right-click the cat in the Sprite List and delete it.

2. Click the **Variables** button and make a variable called "score."

3. Add this code to your sprite. Drag the sprite to the bottom of the Stage.

A If your sprite is too big, put a smaller number here.

B Add the **if ... then** block, then add the **key space pressed?** block on top. Use the drop-down box to select the left arrow.

4. Create another sprite, and add this code to it. Right-click the sprite and choose duplicate. This will make a copy of the sprite and its code.

A Use the **go to x: 0 y: 0** block, then add the **pick random 1 to 10** block on top. Change the numbers to -200 and 200.

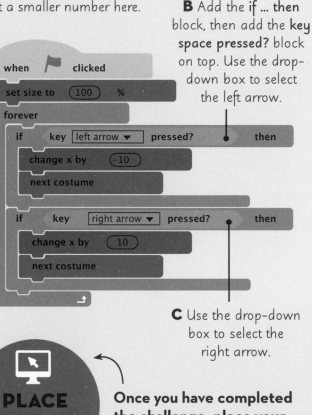

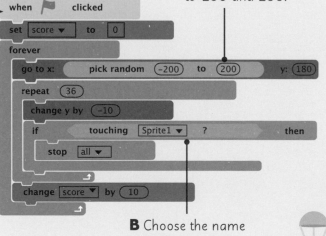

C Use the drop-down box to select the right arrow.

B Choose the name of the sprite you designed. You can see it in the Sprite List.

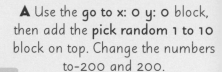

5. Click the green flag to play. The two sprites will fall from the sky. Dodge them using the right and left arrow keys on your keyboard. When you are hit, the game will stop. Keep a track of your score. Can a friend beat it?

PLACE STICKER HERE

Once you have completed the challenge, place your sticker here.

TASK COMPLETE

42

CONGRATULATIONS! You are now a ...

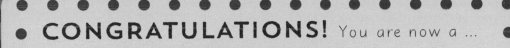

QUALIFIED COMPUTER ARTIST

CODER NAME:

_____

The above-named coder is qualified to be a

COMPUTER ARTIST

and can design characters and create animations in Scratch.

Coder Academy would like to wish you every success in your coding career! GOOD LUCK.

QUALIFICATION DATE:

_____

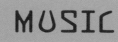
PLAN A TUNE

Music is all about patterns. There are melodies that rise and fall, notes that repeat, and drum rhythms that hold it all together.

If you can make up a pattern, you can code your own music. To start, draw the pattern of notes you want to use. There are two grids on page 45. The top one is for the lead notes (the high notes), and the bottom one is for the bass notes (the low notes).

Look at this example of a tune below. You will use the numbers on the left of the grid for the Scratch activity on page 46, but you can ignore them for now.

C	72
B	71
A	69
G	67
F	65
E	64
D	62
C	60

C	60
B	59
A	57
G	55
F	53
E	52
D	50
C	48

You are going to use the grids below to plan your own tune. Start with the top grid. Work your way from left to right, and fill in one square for each column. The higher up the square is, the higher the note will be. You can leave a column empty if you like. Then do the same with the grid below.

The note names are on the left of each grid to help you if you play an instrument, but you don't need to know them if not.

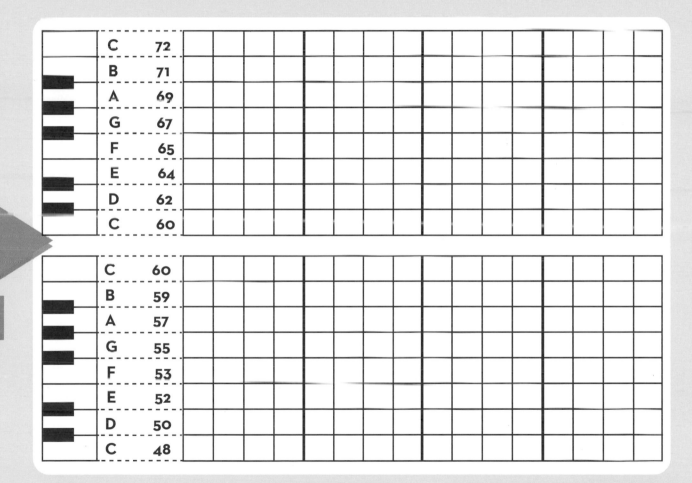

On the following page, you'll learn how to put your tune into Scratch.

Once you have completed the challenge, place your sticker here.

PLACE STICKER HERE

TASK COMPLETE

MUSIC

—CODE—
A TUNE

You are going to use your note patterns on page 45 to code a tune. On the left side of the grids on page 45, a set of numbers accompanies each note. You will put these numbers into two lists in Scratch, and make a short program to play each note in turn.

ENTER YOUR TUNE IN SCRATCH

1. Start a new project. Click the **Variables** button. Click the **Make a List** button and make a list for all sprites called "lead notes."

2. Find the "lead notes" list on the Stage. Click the **+** button at the bottom of it. This will create a text box inside the list.

3. Go to the first column of the top grid on page 45. Look at the first square you filled in. Move your finger left to find the number on that row.

4. Type this number into the box in "lead notes" on the Stage and press Enter. If you left the column empty, type in 0.

5. Go to the second column of the top grid on page 45. Find the second square filled in and add the row number to the second box in the "lead notes" list. Keep going in this way until you've entered all the numbers from the top grid into the "lead notes" list.

6. Click the **Make a List** button and make another list for all sprites called "bass notes."

7. Click the "bass notes" list on the Stage, hold down the mouse button and move the list so it matches the picture below.

8. Repeat steps 2 to 5, but this time, use notes from the bottom grid on page 45 and put the data into the "bass notes" list.

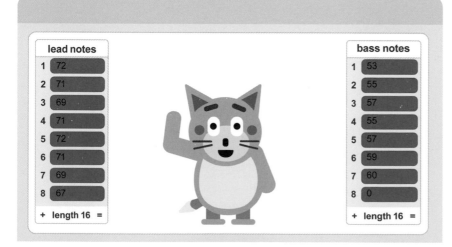

lead notes	
1	72
2	71
3	69
4	71
5	72
6	71
7	69
8	67
+	length 16 =

bass notes	
1	53
2	55
3	57
4	55
5	57
6	59
7	60
8	0
+	length 16 =

CODE YOUR TUNE IN SCRATCH

Now that you have entered your tune data into Scratch, you need to add a program to play it. Follow these steps:

1. Click the **Code** tab. Click the **Add Extension** button in the bottom left of the screen, under the buttons. Click **Music**. This adds the Music blocks to the Blocks Palette.

2. Click the **Variables** button and use **Make a Variable** to create three variables: "beat," "note 1" and "note 2."

3. Add the scripts below to the cat sprite. The scripts don't need to click into each other—add them as they appear here:

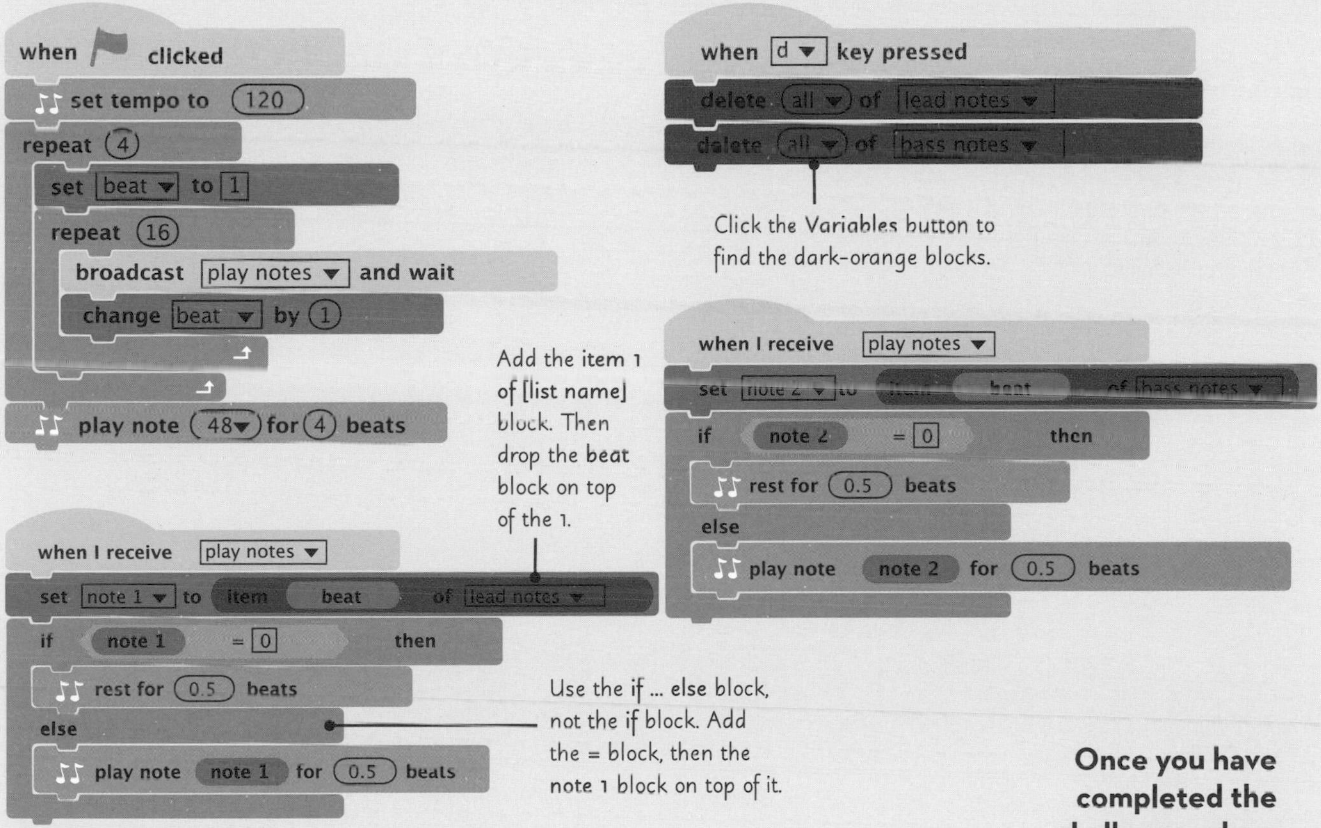

when 🏴 clicked
set tempo to (120)
repeat (4)
  set [beat ▼] to [1]
  repeat (16)
    broadcast [play notes ▼] and wait
    change [beat ▼] by (1)
play note (48▼) for (4) beats

when [d ▼] key pressed
delete (all ▼) of [lead notes ▼]
delete (all ▼) of [bass notes ▼]

Click the Variables button to find the dark-orange blocks.

Add the item 1 of [list name] block. Then drop the **beat** block on top of the 1.

when I receive [play notes ▼]
set [note 2 ▼] to item (beat) of [bass notes ▼]
if (note 2 = [0]) then
  rest for (0.5) beats
else
  play note (note 2) for (0.5) beats

when I receive [play notes ▼]
set [note 1 ▼] to item (beat) of [lead notes ▼]
if (note 1 = [0]) then
  rest for (0.5) beats
else
  play note (note 1) for (0.5) beats

Use the if ... else block, not the if block. Add the = block, then the note 1 block on top of it.

4. Click the green flag to hear your tune.

5. If there's a note you don't like, you can click on it in the list on the Stage to change it.

6. Play around with different numbers to create brand-new tunes! Delete the numbers in the lists by pressing the D key on the keyboard.

Once you have completed the challenge, place your sticker here.

🖱️ **PLACE STICKER HERE**

TASK COMPLETE

—DESIGN AN— INSTRUMENT

You can use Scratch to invent your own instrument. Electronic music often uses sounds from real life, as well as singing and sounds like hand claps. Think of all the different sounds you can record for your instrument to play. Keep a list here:

SOUND LIST

INVENT YOUR OWN INSTRUMENT

You are going to invent a brand-new instrument. It could have strings like a guitar, or be more like a keyboard. Maybe it will be a mixture— or like nothing ever seen before! Give your instrument five buttons or levers to press that each make a different sound. Draw it in the space below. Then, follow the instructions at the bottom of the page to design your instrument in Scratch.

DRAW YOUR INSTRUMENT IN SCRATCH

1. Start a new Scratch project.

2. Hover over the **Choose a Backdrop** button in the bottom right, and click **Paint**.

3. Draw the main body of your instrument, but leave out the buttons.

4. Hover over the **Choose a Sprite** button in the Sprite List, and click **Paint** to paint a new sprite. Draw one of your buttons. It might look like a string, or anything else, but we'll call it a button. Drag it to the right position on the Stage.

5. Draw new sprites for the four other buttons. Turn to page 50 to record the noises for each button.

Once you have completed the challenge, place your sticker here.

PLACE STICKER HERE

TASK COMPLETE

CODE AN INSTRUMENT

A sound designer codes sounds for apps and websites. You are going to record and code a sound for the instrument that you designed on page 49.

RECORD YOUR SOUND

1. Click one of the buttons you designed on page 49 in the Sprite List. Click the **Sounds** tab above the Blocks Palette.

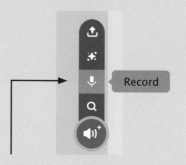

2. Hover over the **Choose a Sound** button in the bottom left and click **Record**. Get ready to make your sound!

3. Click the **circle** button to start recording. Make your sound right away. Press the **square** button to stop recording. Click the **triangle** button to play your sound. If you don't like it, go back to the beginning of step 2 and start again.

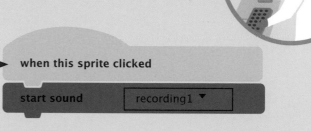

4. Add this code to your sprite. The **start sound** block should contain your last recording, but you can change the recording name if you need to.

5. Try clicking the button you've set up to test that it works. Now add sounds for the remaining four buttons.

You can also use the sounds that come with Scratch. To add one to a sprite, click the Choose a Sound button.

Once you have completed the challenge, place your sticker here.

PLACE STICKER HERE

TASK COMPLETE

CONGRATULATIONS! You are now a ...

QUALIFIED COMPUTER MUSICIAN

CODER NAME:

_____

The above-named coder is qualified to be a

COMPUTER MUSICIAN

and to invent programs using sounds
and compose music for games.

Coder Academy would like to wish you every
success in your coding career! GOOD LUCK.

QUALIFICATION DATE:

_____

WHAT IS HTML?

A trainee website developer needs to learn a computer language called HTML so they can build web pages. HTML uses codes called tags to tell the computer about the different parts of a web page.

HOW TO SPOT TAGS

The tag is always inside angle brackets.

`<h1>This is the title of my web page!</h1>`

There is a tag at the start and at the end of this heading. The end tag has **/** (a forward slash) before it, so the computer knows it's the end tag.

```
<h1>All about dinosaurs</h1>

<p>The dinosaurs lived over 230 million years ago, and they became extinct 66 million years ago.</p>

<p>Or did they? Because scientists have found that today's birds evolved from the dinosaurs.</p>

<p>My top three favorite dinosaurs are:</p>

<ol>

<li>Stegosaurus</li>

<li>Tyrannosaurus rex</li>

<li>Diplodocus</li>

</ol>

<h2>Dinosaur pictures</h2>

<p>Here are some of my favorite dinosaur pictures.</p>

<img src="stegosaurus.jpg">

<img src="rex.jpg">
```

WORD BANK

big heading

list item

picture

small heading

paragraph

ordered list

HTML DETECTIVE

Study the HTML tags in the panel on page 52. Can you guess what instruction each tag gives? Add the correct tags to the boxes in the web page below. Then, using the word bank to help you, write the instruction that each code gives on the dotted lines. A few instructions and tags are already written for you. Some instructions are used more than once.

---

dinosaurs.html

A ( ) # All about dinosaurs ( ) ....big heading....

B (`<p>`) The dinosaurs lived over 230 million years ago, and they became extinct 66 million years ago. ( ) ....

C ( ) Or did they? Because scientists have found that today's birds evolved from the dinosaurs. ( ) ....

D ( ) My top three favorite dinosaurs are: ( ) ....

E ( ) ....ordered list....

F ( ) 1. Stegosaurus ( ) ....

G ( ) 2. Tyrannosaurus rex (`</li>`) ....

H ( ) 3. Diplodocus ( ) ....

I ( ) ....

J ( ) ## Dinosaur pictures ( ) ....

K ( ) Here are some of my favorite dinosaur pictures. ( ) ....

L (`<img>`)

M ( ) ....picture....

Once you have completed the challenge, check your answers below and place your sticker here.

PLACE STICKER HERE

TASK COMPLETE

WEBSITE

— PLAN A —
WEB PAGE

Website content writers plan and create the material for websites. They think about who the website is for and how they can make it stand out, so that it attracts a lot of visitors.

Fill in the blank spaces below and plan a web page all about you. Make it friendly, interesting and fun! We've included the HTML tags, too, but you can ignore them for now.

<h1>All about _____</h1>

<p>Hello! My first name is _____.</p>

<p>I built this web page to tell you about my hobby, which is _____.</p>

Write about your hobby here:

<p>

</p>

Remember: don't include personal information in your web page, such as a phone number, your address or your last name.

```
<p>Here are three surprising things you should know about me:</p>
<ol>
<li>_____</li>
<li>_____</li>
<li>_____</li>
</ol>
```

Do you have a photo of your hobby, or a picture you've made on the computer? You can add it to your web page. Just put its file name in the box below.

```
<p>Here's a picture I made.</p>
<p><img src="_____" width="500"></p>
```

Once you have completed the challenge, place your sticker here.

PLACE STICKER HERE

TASK COMPLETE

— BUILD —
A WEB PAGE

On the previous page, you planned content for a website. As part of your training, you are going to code your content into a computer, to make your own personal web page.

You will need to use a program called a text editor, and save your file as a plain text document. The text editor will be different depending on the computer you use. Here are some examples:
• On Windows, use Notepad. Save as a Text document.
• On a Mac, find TextEdit in Applications. Click the Format menu and choose Make Plain Text.

```
<!DOCTYPE html>
<html>
<body>
Hello, world!
</body>
</html>
```

1. Type this code into your text editor. The code tells the web browser (the program you use to view websites on the Internet) that the file is using HTML. The <body> tags are used for the start and end of the main page content.

2. Save your file on the desktop with the file name mypage.html. Don't put .txt or anything else on the end. Double click your file to open it in a web browser. You should see just the words "Hello, world!" in the browser.

3. Delete "Hello, world!" in the text editor program. Go to your web page plan on pages 54-55. Type in everything from your plan, including the tags and the content. Make sure that everything is between the <body> and </body> tags.

4. If you're using an image, save it in the same place as your "mypage.html" file.

5. Save your "mypage.html" file and double click it on the desktop. You should see your very own web page, all about you. Try making different web pages. How about making one to show a friend?

<<<<<<<<<<<<<<<<<<<<<

If your code isn't working, check those angle brackets. If you need to fix it, remember to save your web page and reload it in the browser.

<<<<<<<<<<<<<<<<<<<<<

If you don't want to type so much, or if you can't get it working, you can download a ready-made file from www.sean.co.uk/books/coder and fill in the blanks.

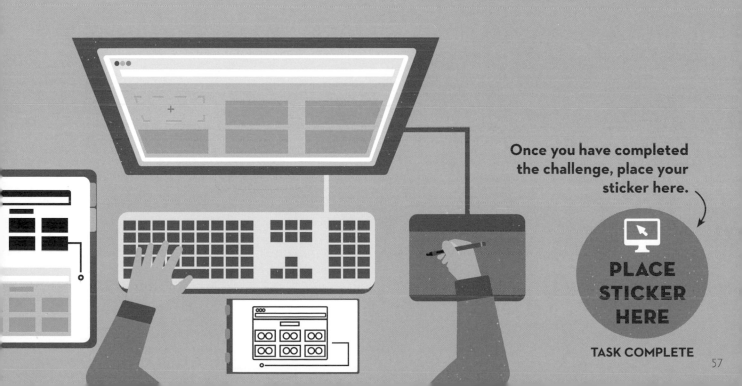

Once you have completed the challenge, place your sticker here.

PLACE STICKER HERE

TASK COMPLETE

COLOR CODES

Once a web designer has set up a web page, the next job is to make it look good for visitors to the site. The simplest way to do this is to add color.

HTML describes colors using a number system called hexadecimal. It uses the same numbers as we do, but it also uses the first six letters of the alphabet. The table below shows you how to count to 15 in hexadecimal. Our normal counting numbers, called the decimal system, are on the top row:

DECIMAL	0	1	2	3	4	5	6	7	8	9	10	11	12	13	14	15
HEXADECIMAL	0	1	2	3	4	5	6	7	8	9	A	B	C	D	E	F

In hexadecimal, the A means ten, the B means eleven and so on. Hexadecimal allows computers to process large numbers with as few characters as possible. For example, in the decimal system, 15 is written with two characters, but in hexadecimal, only one character is used: F.

The table on the right shows you hex codes that computers use for different colors. You can make any shade of color you want by using different combinations of the hexadecimal numbers—similar to mixing paint.

COLOR CODE	COLOR NAME
#FF0000	Bright red
#00FF00	Bright green
#FFFF00	Yellow
#0000FF	Bright blue
#CC00EE	Purple
#00FFFF	Cyan
#FFFFFF	White
#000000	Black

COLOR-BY-HEX

You are going to use the hex codes to color the image below. Check the numbers on the picture against the table on page 58. Find the hex code and its color. Then, shade each section with the matching colored pen or pencil.

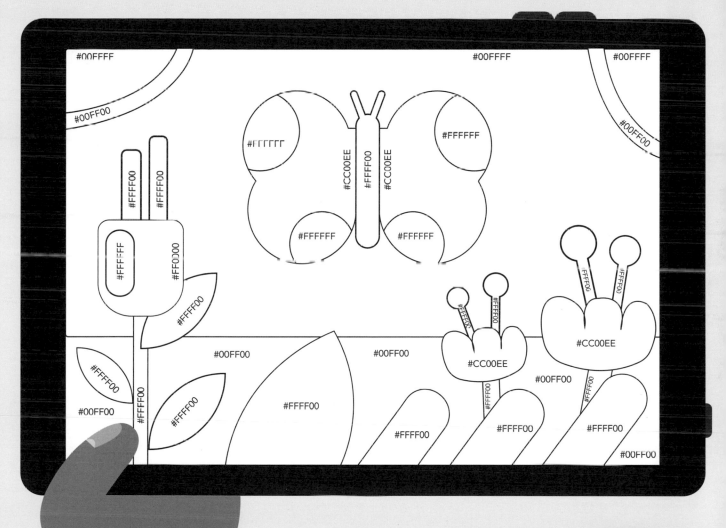

Once you have completed the challenge, place your sticker here.

PLACE STICKER HERE

TASK COMPLETE

WEBSITE

—DECORATE—
A WEB PAGE

You are going to add some colors to your web page. Start by changing the heading. Find the <h1> tag in your code, and add this code to it:

`<h1 style="color:#00FF00; background:#000000;">All about coding</h1>`

HERE'S WHAT THE CODE MEANS

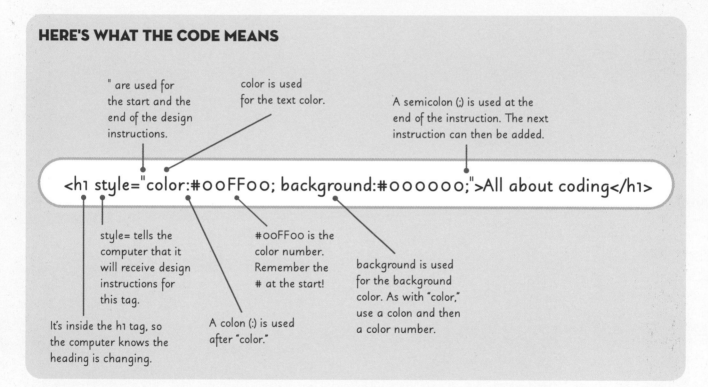

" are used for the start and the end of the design instructions.

color is used for the text color.

A semicolon (;) is used at the end of the instruction. The next instruction can then be added.

`<h1 style="color:#00FF00; background:#000000;">All about coding</h1>`

style= tells the computer that it will receive design instructions for this tag.

It's inside the h1 tag, so the computer knows the heading is changing.

A colon (:) is used after "color."

#00FF00 is the color number. Remember the # at the start!

background is used for the background color. As with "color," use a colon and then a color number.

Save your file, and double click it to open it again in your browser. It should look like this:

All about coding

Remember to load your web page in your browser again to see the change.

Experiment with color numbers from page 58 or make up your own. They should be six digits, but you can use any mix of the numbers 0 to 9 and the letters A to F.

You can add a border to your heading, or to any of your paragraphs, too. Add a border around your first paragraph. When you add a border style, you give the computer three bits of information:

The border color

```
<p style="border:5px #CC99CC dashed;"> Hello! I am a coder.</p>
```

The border size in pixels   The type of line

It should look like this:

All about coding

Hello! I am a coder.

Try different colored and sized lines, on this paragraph or on other paragraphs. You can try other types of line, too. Choose from solid, dotted, dashed, double, groove, ridge, inset and outset. Remember to reopen your page in your browser each time you make a change.

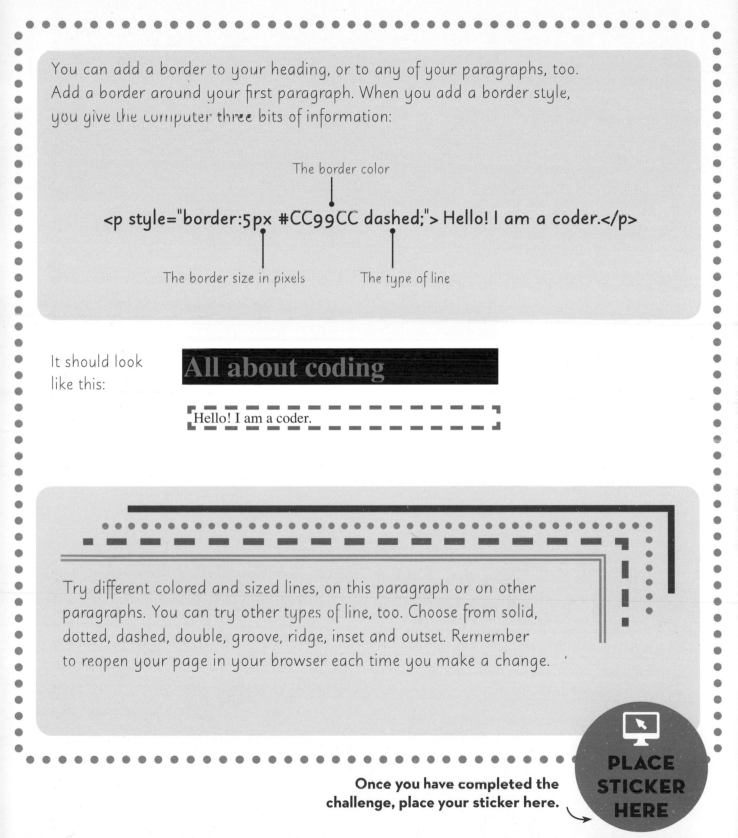

Once you have completed the challenge, place your sticker here.

PLACE STICKER HERE

TASK COMPLETE

61

CONGRATULATIONS! You are now a ...

QUALIFIED WEBSITE DESIGNER

CODER NAME:

_____

The above-named coder is qualified to be a

WEBSITE DESIGNER

and to create the code and
design for websites.

Coder Academy would like to wish you
every success in your career! GOOD LUCK.

QUALIFICATION DATE:

_____

WELL DONE!

You have successfully completed all your
tasks and finished your coder training.

You are now ready to graduate from the Coder Academy.

As part of your graduation ceremony, you should read
the coder's code below and promise to follow it.

**ONCE YOU HAVE DONE THIS, YOU CAN
SIGN YOUR NAME BELOW.**

1. As a coder, I know that people rely on my programs. I will test them to make sure they work correctly, and fix any errors people tell me about.

2. To be a good coder, I need to keep developing my skills. I will continue to learn about coding, and continue to make new programs.

3. I will look at other people's code to see if I can figure out how it works, and I will let other people look at my code so they can learn, too.

4. Whether I'm making my own program, or typing one in from a book, I will always experiment and try new things to see if I can make my programs even better.

5. When using the Internet, I will stay safe. I will make sure I don't share any personal information, and I will ask for help if I see anything that makes me uncomfortable.

Draw or glue a
picture of your
face here.

SIGN HERE:

_ _ _ _ _ _ _ _ _ _ _ _ _ _ _ _ _ _

CODER'S KIT

- 2 model robots
  (on the flaps of the book)
- Stickers
- Coding Pairs cards
- Coding Careers poster
- Robot Programming
  Challenge game

CODING PAIRS
(2 PLAYERS)

1. Shuffle the cards, then place them in a row, face-down on a flat surface.
2. Take turns to flip over two cards of your choice. If they are a matching pair, keep them. If not, turn the cards over and let the next player take their turn.
3. The player to collect the most pairs is the winner.

ROBOT PROGRAMMING CHALLENGE
(2 PLAYERS)

Find the game board on the pull-out at the back of the book. Push out the dice, then fold and glue it together. Push out the target. Follow the instructions on the inner flaps to assemble the robots.

1. Lay the game board flat on a table, maze-side up. Each player chooses a robot. Decide who goes first.
2. The first player rolls the dice and places their robot on the matching row number.
3. The player rolls again and moves their robot to the matching column number.
4. The player repeats steps 2 and 3 to place the target into the maze.
5. The player writes a list of instructions to move the robot to the target. The only instructions that can be used are: GO FORWARD ONE SQUARE, ROTATE LEFT and ROTATE RIGHT.
6. The second player moves the first player's robot to the target using the written instructions. If the instructions are wrong (the robot hits a wall), the robot must stop.
7. The second player takes their turn, following steps 2 to 6. The player whose robot gets closest to the target is the winner.